Y STATE!

NEVADA

Terry Allan Hicks

Ellen H. Todras

Cavendish
Square

New York

Published in 2014 by Cavendish Square Publishing, LLC
303 Park Avenue South, Suite 1247, New York, NY 10010

Library of Congress Cataloging-in-Publication Data
Hicks, Terry Allan.
        Nevada / Terry Allan Hicks. — 2nd ed.
          p. cm. — (It's my state!)
        Summary: Surveys the history, geography, government, economy, and people of Nevada — Provided by publisher.
        Includes bibliographical references and index.
        ISBN 978-0-7614-8000-6 (hardcover) —ISBN 978-1-62712-101-9 (paperback)— ISBN 978-0-7614-8007-5 (ebook)
        1. Nevada—Juvenile literature. I. Title.
    F841.3.H53 2014
    979.3—dc23   2012024118

This edition developed for Cavendish Square Publishing by RJF Publishing LLC (www.RJFpublishing.com)
Series Designer, Second Edition: Tammy West/Westgraphix LLC

CONTENTS

State Tree: Single-Leaf Piñon

This tough, hardy pine thrives even in the coarse, rocky soil of the high mountains. The tree's pine nuts were once an important food source for the American Indians of the region and are still used in many recipes today.

State Bird: Mountain Bluebird

Mountain bluebirds live in the high-country regions of Nevada. They eat insects, such as grasshoppers and crickets, and often hover in the air while feeding.

State Animal: Desert Bighorn Sheep

The desert bighorn—also known as the Nelson sheep—is well adapted to life in Nevada, because it can go a long time without water. An adult male may stand around 4 feet (1.2 meters) tall and weigh 175 pounds (80 kilograms). The males have long, heavy, curving horns that they use to fight other males during mating season. The females have shorter spiky horns.

State Flower: Sagebrush

Sagebrush, which has pale yellow flowers and a sweet smell, can grow in places where conditions are too harsh for other plants. In the winter, sagebrush may be the only food Nevada's cattle and sheep can find on the open range. The American Indians of Nevada have used sagebrush to make items as varied as medicine and candles.

State Rock: Sandstone

Sandstone is found throughout Nevada. There are sandstone peaks and walls at Red Rock Canyon National Conservation Area. Sandstone is often used as a building material. The state capitol is made of this native rock.

State Fossil: Ichthyosaur

Hundreds of millions of years ago, these now-extinct reptiles swam in warm, shallow saltwater seas that covered what is now the Nevada desert. Many ichthyosaur (*Shonisaurus popularis*) fossils—the remains or traces of plants or animals from an earlier time—have been found around Berlin, in the central part of the state. The ichthyosaur was named the official state fossil in 1977.

NEVADA

Owyhee

Owyhee
Desert

SILK CREEK MOUNTAINS

Black Rock
Desert

QUINN RIVER

THE LAVA
BEDS

Winnemucca

HUMBOLDT RIVER

Battle
Mountain

Pyramid
Lake

Humboldt
Salt Marsh

INDEPENDENCE MOUNTAINS

Elko
Spring Creek

West
Wendover

HUNTINGTON RIVER

RUBY MOUNTAINS

Eureka

Sparks

Reno

Carson
City

Lake
Tahoe

Walker
Lake

Hawthorne

EXCELSIOR MOUNTAINS

Boundary
Peak

TOIYABE RANGE

MONITOR RANGE

HUMBOLDT-
TOIYABE
NATIONAL
FOREST

Tonopah

Lunar Crater

Ruth
Copper
Pit

Ely

Caliente

DEATH
VALLEY
NATIONAL
PARK

Nevada
Test
Site

DESERT NATIONAL
WILDLIFE RANGE

DELMAR MOUNTAINS

Mesquite

Beatty

Amargosa Desert

VIVA

Las
Vegas

Lake Mead

HOOVER
DAM

Boulder
City

Laughlin

COLORADO RIVER

N

W   E

S

The Silver State

With snowcapped mountains, clear lakes, and large stretches of desert where wild horses roam, Nevada is one of the most beautiful states in the United States. For centuries, because the harsh climate made settling difficult, this area was nearly empty of inhabitants. But in recent years, millions of people have discovered Nevada, making it one of the nation's great tourist attractions and one of the fastest-growing states in population.

Nevada is a huge state—the seventh largest in the country—with a land area of 109,781 square miles (284,331 square kilometers). The state is divided into seventeen counties. Even though Nevada is a large state in land area, it ranks thirty-fifth in population. Its residents are not evenly distributed on the land. More than half of Nevadans live in the state's five most-populous cities.

The Sierra Nevada

The state of Nevada takes its name from the Sierra Nevada, the great mountain range that runs north-south through parts of eastern California and western Nevada. The Sierra Nevada began to form about 150 million years ago, when huge masses of rock began to shift and push upward and volcanoes spewed molten

Quick Facts

NEVADA BORDERS

North	Oregon
	Idaho
South	California
East	Arizona
	Utah
West	California

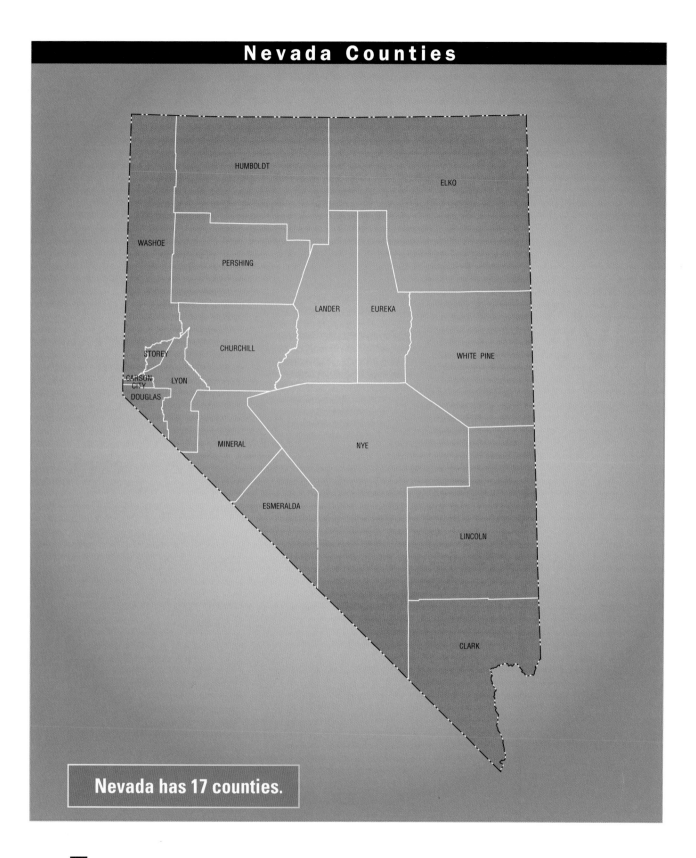

Nevada Counties

HUMBOLDT

ELKO

WASHOE

PERSHING

LANDER

EUREKA

CHURCHILL

STOREY

WHITE PINE

CARSON CITY

LYON

DOUGLAS

MINERAL

NYE

ESMERALDA

LINCOLN

CLARK

Nevada has 17 counties.

The name of the Sierra Nevada mountain range comes from the Spanish language. *Sierra* means "mountain" in Spanish, and *nevada* is Spanish for "snow-covered."

lava that cooled to form granite mountains. The tall peaks of the Sierra Nevada create a natural barrier between Nevada and California. The highest point in Nevada, Boundary Peak, at 13,147 feet (4,007 m), lies very close to the border between the two states.

Nevada has never been an easy place to live. The difficulty of traveling through the Sierra Nevada discouraged settlers for many years. Even today, with modern highways and four-wheel-drive vehicles, heavy snows sometimes cut off entire towns for days or even weeks at a time. And yet, American Indians have made the Sierra Nevada their home for thousands of years. This is also the part of present-day Nevada where settlement by people of European descent began.

The strip of western Nevada in the shadow of the Sierra Nevada is where Reno, also known as the "biggest little city in the world," is located. Reno has only about 225,000 residents, but an average of more than 350,000 visitors travel to the city each month. Most of them come to enjoy an industry that has been the backbone of the state's economy for more than half a century: gambling.

But this part of Nevada has much more than roulette wheels, slot machines, and card tables to offer. Tourists remember Nevada's rich past in places such as Virginia City, which works hard to preserve the mining heritage that served as inspiration for the nickname the Silver State. More than a hundred years ago, when Virginia City was a very prosperous silver mining town, its population was around 30,000. Fewer than one thousand people live there today.

Reno is a year-round vacation spot.

A DEEP, CLEAR LAKE

Lake Tahoe is high in the Sierra Nevada mountain range—6,229 feet (1,899 m) above sea level. Located partly in Nevada and partly in California, it is one of the deepest, clearest lakes in the world. The lake's lowest spot is 1,645 feet (501 m) down. Lake Tahoe never freezes over due partly to its size and partly to currents that keep the water moving.

Just 15 miles (24 km) south of Virginia City is another former mining center, Carson City. This tourist destination offers museums and restored buildings from pioneer days. Carson City is also Nevada's capital. Lawmakers meet here to decide on important issues facing the state.

West of Carson City, along the California-Nevada state line, is Lake Tahoe. The lake, famous for its sparkling blue water, covers 193 square miles (500 sq km). It is said that the water is so clear you can sometimes see objects 75 feet (23 m) below the surface. Resorts on the shores of Lake Tahoe draw boaters, swimmers, and hikers in the summer. In the winter, skiers and snowboarders come to enjoy the deep powder at Mount Rose or Diamond Peak.

The Great Basin

Most of Nevada is in a region known as the Great Basin, about 190,000 square miles (492,000 sq km) in size. The Great Basin stretches from the foothills of the Sierra Nevada, on the state's western border, all the way to the Rocky Mountains, on Nevada's eastern border. This low-lying area was formed millions of years ago,

Mount Grant and Walker Lake are part of the Great Basin region.

when movements within Earth raised the surrounding areas higher. The Great Basin is shaped like a huge bowl, which is how it got its name. It is known for its unusual drainage system. Rivers and streams flowing into the Great Basin from the surrounding mountains end in low, marshy areas called sinks or in stretches of dry, cracked clay called playas.

Nevada has more than a dozen volcanic areas in the Great Basin, the best known of which is the Lunar Crater Volcanic Field. It is more than 100 square miles (260 sq km) in size, located at the southern end of the Pancake Range mountains. The 430-foot-deep (130-m-deep) Lunar Crater has been designated a National Natural Landmark.

The Great Basin also includes part of the Mojave Desert. This desert—the hottest and driest in the United States—covers more than 25,000 square miles (65,000 sq km) in southern Nevada and southeastern California. Desert bighorn sheep, desert tortoises, and jackrabbits live in much of the sparsely populated Mojave. The city of Las Vegas lies in this arid region as well.

The northern section of Nevada is "cowboy country," where many ranchers still drive their herds on horseback. Sometimes, ranchers and their herds stop traffic on the highways on the way to and from the ranches. The area around Elko, in the northeastern corner of the state, also has huge open-pit mining operations. The region has some of the largest gold deposits in the world.

Stretching south from cowboy country is a huge expanse of flatlands. Much of this area is semidesert—dry land where only the toughest plants and animals can survive. Cutting across this area are more than a hundred small, steep-sided mountain ranges that run from north to south. Very few people live here, and some counties are almost uninhabited. A stretch of Highway 50, outside Fallon, is sometimes called "the loneliest road in America," because people can drive parts of it for hours without seeing any other human beings.

GREAT BASIN NATIONAL PARK

Great Basin National Park, created in 1986, is the only U.S. national park located entirely in Nevada. Visitors to the park can climb Wheeler Peak, 13,063 feet (3,982 m) high. They can also explore the spectacular underground rock formations of the Lehman Caves (right) and walk on a glacier. Great Basin National Park's isolated location, far from any brightly lit cities, makes it one of the darkest places in the country after sunset. For this reason, it is a great place to observe the night sky.

But this does not mean there is no human activity in the Nevada countryside. The federal government owns huge stretches of the Silver State, which it uses for many different purposes, such as designing ways to dispose of dangerous materials.

Why are parts of Nevada so empty? Large areas of the state just do not have enough water to support a large population. But in the southern Nevada desert, a huge body of water can be found. The water comes from the Hoover Dam, located along the Nevada-Arizona border. This enormous concrete dam controls the flooding of the Colorado River and supplies precious water for homes and farms. When the Hoover Dam was built in the 1930s, it created Lake Mead, a reservoir in the desert. This body of water, located partly in Nevada and partly in Arizona, is one of the largest artificial lakes in the world. It covers about 157,900 acres (63,900 hectares).

Today, millions of people come every year to enjoy this clear blue lake in the middle of the bone-dry desert. Power generators at the Hoover Dam also produce large amounts of electricity. That is a good thing because rising from the desert only about 25 miles (40 km) to the northwest are the glittering neon-lit towers of Las Vegas.

Las Vegas, located in southern Nevada, is the largest city in the state. It is home to the world-famous Las Vegas Strip—a stretch of 4 miles (6 km) of road lined with hotels and casinos. Las Vegas is often called the Entertainment Capital of the World. Many singers, dancers, circus professionals, and other entertainers perform on the stages of this city.

Many people have come to the Las Vegas area to live and work. In the decade from 2000 to 2010, it was the fastest-growing metropolitan area in the United States, according to the U.S. Census Bureau, even though it was hit hard by the economic downturn, or recession, that began in late 2007. What was once a small, sleepy town now extends far out into what had been uninhabitable desert.

Las Vegas Boulevard South is also known as the Las Vegas Strip.

THE ET HIGHWAY

Nevada State Highway 375 runs for 98 miles (158 km) in south-central Nevada. In 1996, it was officially named the Extraterrestrial Highway because of the many Unidentified Flying Objects, or UFOs, reported on the road. It is true that the ET Highway passes near a mysterious U.S. military base called Area 51, which seems to be used by the federal government for highly classified programs. Some people speculate that Area 51 holds alien spacecraft that crashed in the nearby desert, while others believe a lack of information encourages imaginations to run wild.

Climate

The Silver State has one of the world's most extreme climates. Nevada is the driest state in the country. Its average precipitation totals just 7 inches (18 centimeters) a year. The national average is 40 inches (102 cm). Yet some parts of the Sierra Nevada get more than 80 inches (200 cm) of precipitation in a year. And in many parts of the state, sudden thunderstorms send flash floods racing down on unsuspecting hikers.

Temperatures in the state also vary. The temperature in the south can shift wildly in a single day, from 80 degrees Fahrenheit (27 degrees Celsius) in the afternoon to only a few degrees above freezing—32 °F (0 °C)—at night. The desert town of Laughlin recorded a blistering 125 °F (52 °C) on June 29, 1994. But Nevada also experiences cold temperatures. The coldest temperature recorded was on January 8, 1937, when thermometers in the northern town of San Jacinto fell to a bone-chilling –50 °F (–46 °C).

Despite these wide variations in temperature and precipitation, Nevada's climate is very consistent in one way: There is almost always a lot of sunlight. In

fact, the state's southern desert can get as many as 320 sunny days in a year.

Wild Nevada

Many plants and animals survive—and even thrive—in Nevada, despite the harsh environment. Even in the parched desert, sagebrush, yucca, Joshua trees, and more than two dozen types of cactus can be found. In places in the state where water is more plentiful, Indian paintbrush, shooting stars, and yellow and white violets dot the countryside.

Many parts of the Silver State are almost completely treeless, but juniper, pine, and fir trees grow in the mountains. Ancient bristlecone pines cling to the steep slopes of Wheeler Peak, in Great Basin National Park. All over the state, wherever there is a little water, alder, chokecherry, and cottonwood trees grow. In the autumn, their leaves turn yellow, bringing a welcome touch of color to the landscape.

Bright, colorful wildflowers grow in the Humboldt-Toiyabe National Forest.

The Gila monster feeds on small mammals, birds, and eggs.

Among the large animals in Nevada are bighorn sheep, pronghorns (which are sometimes called antelope), elk, mule deer, mustangs, and small donkeys called burros. Coyotes and bobcats are also common. Smaller animals include cottontail rabbits, foxes, and porcupines. Nevada also has plenty of reptiles, including lizards and snakes, such as the Western fence lizard, the rattlesnake, and the poisonous Gila monster.

Many parts of Nevada are growing so fast that humans sometimes come into conflict with wildlife. Coyotes have been known to drink from suburban swimming pools, and rattlesnakes sometimes sleep under cars on hot days.

Nevada's lakes and rivers are filled with fish that sport fishers love to catch and eat, including largemouth bass, perch, and trout. Many birds—including a number of waterbirds, such as ducks, geese, and pelicans—fill Nevada's skies. Nevada is also home to birds of prey such as falcons, bald and golden eagles, and owls, as well as smaller birds such as bluebirds, hummingbirds, and doves.

Wildlife at Risk

Nevada's fast-growing human population threatens the habitats of some of its plants and animals. An animal or plant type, or species, is considered threatened when it is at risk of becoming endangered. When a species is endangered, it is at risk of dying out in its range or a large area of its range.

Nevada has twenty-five endangered and fifteen threatened species. The state reptile, the desert tortoise, is threatened. This reptile, the largest in the southwestern United States, can live more than seventy years. It survives in the harsh conditions of southern Nevada—hot in the summer, cold in the winter—by living in underground burrows. Nevada's desert tortoise population has fallen sharply in recent years. Some people hunt the animals illegally, and others hit them accidentally with their cars.

The cui-ui (pronounced kwee-wee), a rare fish found only in Pyramid Lake, has been listed as an endangered species since 1967. Other endangered animals in Nevada include the gray wolf, the Southwestern willow flycatcher, and many more kinds of fish. Endangered plants in the state include the herbs steamboat buckwheat and Amargosa niterwort.

The Nevada Fish and Wildlife Office is a state agency whose mission is to conserve Nevada's natural biological diversity. The agency works with many partners to prevent native species throughout the state from dying out and to help increase the populations of endangered species.

Many Nevadans are concerned about the need to protect their unique natural environment. For example, the state legislature has passed important laws to protect Nevada's wild horses, keep Lake Tahoe free from pollution, and set aside large wilderness areas as nature preserves. The people of Nevada are determined to protect their clean air and valuable water from the damaging effects of pollution and development.

An adult desert tortoise can survive as long as a year without water.

American White Pelican

Every spring, thousands of American white pelicans descend on the streams and lakes of western Nevada, especially Pyramid Lake, to breed. These waterbirds can be 50 inches (125 cm) long. Their wingspan can measure 110 inches (280 cm). The birds catch fish in their huge beaks while swimming. When the weather turns cold, they head south with their young.

Bristlecone Pine

The bristlecone is a tough pine tree with sharp needles and prickly cones. It grows in the high mountains of Nevada and California. Bristlecone pines may be the oldest living things on Earth. In 1964, one bristlecone believed to have been more than four thousand years old was cut down on the slopes of Wheeler Peak.

Yucca

Yuccas are tall plants that grow throughout the southern Nevada desert. They have white or purple flowers and tall, spiky leaves that store water for the plant to use during dry periods. American Indians ate the flowers and leaves of the yucca. The plant's roots can be made into soap.

Wild Horse

In Nevada's pioneer days, horses sometimes escaped from their owners to live in the wild. These horses—often called mustangs—remained wild, traveled in herds, and bred together. Today, as many as 2,500 of their wild descendants roam free in the state's wide-open spaces.

Mule Deer

The mule deer takes its name from its large mulelike ears, which move constantly. This desert dweller has an excellent sense of smell, which helps it find water underground. Using its large hooves, the mule deer can dig as deep as 2 feet (60 cm) down for water.

Sidewinder

The poisonous sidewinder, one of seven rattlesnake species in Nevada, is named for the unusual way it moves. It moves its body sideways in a looping motion, making a distinctive S-shaped mark in the sand.

From the Beginning

Nevada's climate and terrain make it challenging to live in the Silver State. Yet American Indians have lived in the region for thousands of years, and other groups have been coming since the late 1700s.

The First Nevadans

The first people who lived in the area that includes present-day Nevada were early American Indians, now known as Paleo-Indians. They are believed to have been descendants of people who crossed a land bridge that once connected Asia and North America tens of thousands of years ago. Over time, they spread out all over the Americas. The Paleo-Indians left behind many traces of their way of life, including stone weapons, baskets, and sandals. They also left behind rock carvings called petroglyphs. These artifacts show that the Paleo-Indians were living in the area as early as 10,000 BCE.

Then, between 300 BCE and 100 CE, a different group of American Indian people, known as the Ancestral Puebloans (Anasazi), came to the region. It is not clear where this group came from. By about 700 CE, the Ancestral Puebloans were

Quick Facts

NEVADA ROCK CARVINGS
Eight petroglyph sites in Nevada are listed on the National Register of Historic Places. Some of these sites have hundreds of petroglyphs, many dating back about one thousand years.

The Valley of Fire State Park, near Overton, features drawings carved into sandstone by Ancestral Puebloans more than one thousand years ago.

building communal dwellings called pueblos in several areas of the Southwest. The elaborate multistoried buildings, made out of sun-dried clay bricks, had as many as one hundred rooms. The largest Ancestral Puebloan community may have been home to almost 20,000 people.

The Ancestral Puebloans were farmers. They built dams on the rivers to irrigate, or bring water to, their fields of beans, corn, and squash. Skilled artists, they created beautiful black-and-white pottery and intricately woven baskets now often part of museum collections.

By about 1150 CE, these remarkable people simply disappeared. Did famine, or drought, or war with neighboring American Indians drive them out? The question has fascinated archaeologists and historians for many years, but nobody knows the answer.

During the early sixteenth century, the region that includes present-day Nevada was inhabited by American Indians unrelated to the Ancestral Puebloans. The Northern Paiute lived in what is now western Nevada, while the Southern Paiute lived in the southeastern portion. The Shoshone made their homes in the eastern and central sections of present-day Nevada. The Washoe lived around the Lake Tahoe region.

Most of these peoples were nomadic hunters and gatherers. They traveled across the mountains and deserts in search of food. They followed herds of animals and hunted pronghorns and bighorn sheep. They also trapped rabbits and waterbirds, and they ate pine nuts and other plants. The American Indian way of life remained unchanged for centuries, until European explorers and settlers began to arrive.

Exploration

The first European explorer to set foot in the region was probably Father Francisco Garcés, a Spanish priest who passed through while traveling from New Mexico to California in 1776. The Spaniards claimed the region that now includes Nevada as theirs, but they never really established settlements there. In 1821, when Mexico gained its independence from Spain, what is now Nevada became part of Mexico.

Other explorers passed through the area in the early 1800s, but they never stayed long. In 1827, Jedediah Smith, an American mountain man, led a party of fur trappers from today's Utah on the difficult journey across Nevada to California and back again. John Charles Frémont, a U.S. Army officer and mapmaker, crisscrossed present-day Nevada in 1843 and 1844. He named Carson River after his guide, the frontiersman Christopher "Kit" Carson.

John Charles Frémont, born in 1813 in Savannah, Georgia, was an explorer of the western United States.

EARLY ROUTE TO CALIFORNIA

The Old Spanish Trail, which cuts through southern Nevada, was one of the earliest routes west to southern California. It linked Santa Fe, New Mexico, and Los Angeles, California, at a time when the Southwest belonged to Mexico. Between 1830 and 1840, Mexican and American traders used mule trains on the Old Spanish Trail to bring woolen goods to California. They returned with mules and horses for the Missouri and New Mexico markets.

Settling the West

In 1846, the United States went to war with Mexico. The United States won the Mexican-American War, and the Treaty of Guadalupe Hidalgo officially ended the war in 1848. This agreement gave the United States control of most of the Southwest, including the land that is now Nevada. By then, thousands of American settlers were already headed west in wagon trains, to settle in Oregon and California. Beginning in 1849, even more came after gold was discovered at Sutter's Mill in northern California. Suddenly, people began pouring into the California gold fields. Many of them used a route that passed through present-day Nevada. It was a long and dangerous trip.

In 1850, the U.S. Congress created the Utah Territory—a large area of land that included most of present-day Nevada. Some of the first white settlers in this territory were members of a religious group known as the Mormons. Mormons began

Mormons traveled west to the Utah Territory using handcarts to transport their supplies and luggage.

settling there with the goal of practicing their religion in peace. One group of Mormons founded a trading post called Mormon Station in the Carson Valley in 1851. It was the first permanent settlement by people of European descent in the land that would become Nevada.

In 1859, two prospectors found an enormous vein of gold running beneath the Sierra Nevada. Before they could file their claim to the land, they died. Another prospector, Henry Comstock, swore he owned the land where they had found the gold. Although he sold his claim and died a poor man, the find is called the Comstock Lode.

The discovery set off another gold rush, but the prospectors working the Comstock soon made an even more amazing discovery. The gold they were digging up was mixed with a blue-black "mud." They complained about the mud, until someone realized it contained silver. The silver was worth far more than the original gold. It was, in fact, the richest silver deposit in the United States.

When the news of the silver strike reached others, even more fortune seekers began flooding into the region. Scratching for silver in the rocky ground was hard, dirty, dangerous work. Many men died from mining accidents, disease, or harsh weather. The 1859–1860 winter was especially severe. Heavy snow closed the Sierra Nevada passes, and food supplies could not get through. The silver fields were also dangerous because they were lawless places. Disputes were often settled with fists, knives, or guns.

Miners in Virginia City remove some of the Comstock Lode's rich deposits after gold and silver were discovered there in 1859.

Despite these hardships, entire towns grew up practically overnight. Virginia City, which had been little more than a few prospectors' tents in 1859, had a population of more than 14,000 by 1870. The city even had its own newspaper, the *Territorial Enterprise*. A young reporter for the *Enterprise*, Samuel Clemens, later became world-famous as Mark Twain, author of *The Adventures of Tom Sawyer* and *Adventures of Huckleberry Finn*. Twain also published a book about his experiences in the West, including an account of the silver strike and of people's passion for the beautiful metal.

In Their Own Words

I would have been more or less than human if I had not gone mad like the rest. Cartloads of solid silver bricks, as large as pigs of lead, were arriving from the mills every day, and such sights as that gave substance to the wild talk about me. I succumbed and grew as frenzied as the craziest.

—Mark Twain (Samuel Clemens), *Roughing It* (1872)

By 1880, Virginia City had lumber mills, churches, hotels, and public schools.

The silver rush brought many white settlers to what is now Nevada. The settlers and the American Indians did not always understand one another's ways.

The silver rush and the increase in white settlement brought trouble for the region's American Indians. The prospectors often stole the Indians' land, hunted the Indians' game, and cut down the trees that the Indians used for tools, shelter, and food. This sometimes led to violence between the two groups.

In 1860, a group of Paiute Indians—angered by the kidnapping of two young girls from their village—killed three white men. The white settlers put together a group to fight the Paiute. But the Paiute ambushed them near Pyramid Lake. Seventy-six settlers were killed, in the first engagement of what came to be called the Pyramid Lake War. The settlers recovered and, aided by U.S. Army troops, killed about 160 Paiute. The war lasted only a few months, and it ended American Indian resistance in Nevada forever. The federal government forced the American Indians of Nevada to move to reservations that had been set aside for them. One Nevada group, the Northern Paiute, refused to live on a reservation and settled on wilderness lands in what is now southern Utah instead.

MAKING A PIONEER SUNBONNET

Pioneers heading west in wagon trains made simple hats and bonnets to protect themselves from the sun and dust. By following these instructions, you can make a bonnet.

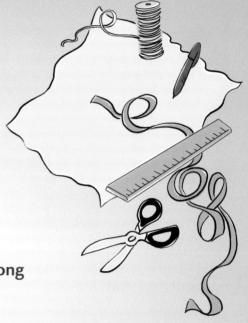

WHAT YOU NEED

Newspapers or old magazines

Piece of cotton or linen fabric, about
20 by 20 inches (50 by 50 cm)

Ruler

Pen

String, thread, or twine, 1 foot (30 cm) long

Scissors

Ribbon, 4 feet (1.2 m) long by about $\frac{1}{2}$ inch (1 cm) wide

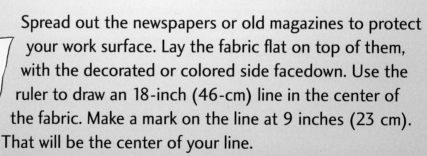

Spread out the newspapers or old magazines to protect your work surface. Lay the fabric flat on top of them, with the decorated or colored side facedown. Use the ruler to draw an 18-inch (46-cm) line in the center of the fabric. Make a mark on the line at 9 inches (23 cm). That will be the center of your line.

Tie the string to the pen. Make sure that the distance from the end of the string to the pen is only 9 inches (23 cm). Hold the end of the string without the pen at the center mark on your line.

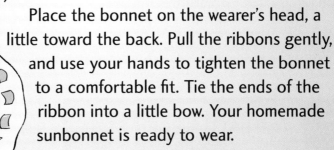

Stretch out the string so that it is straight and use the pen to draw a circle on your fabric. The edges of your circle should touch the ends of the 18-inch (46-cm) line. Cut out your circle with the scissors.

Using the ruler and pen, make marks around the circle, about 1$\frac{1}{2}$ inches (4 cm) from the edge. Make the marks about 1 inch (2.5 cm) long and leave a space of about 1 inch (2.5 cm) between each mark. Cut a narrow slit on each mark, just wide enough to fit the ribbon through.

Turn the fabric over so that the outer side is facing you. Weave the ribbon through the slits, alternating over and under. You should leave 3 or 4 inches (8 or 10 cm) at both ends of the ribbon.

Place the bonnet on the wearer's head, a little toward the back. Pull the ribbons gently, and use your hands to tighten the bonnet to a comfortable fit. Tie the ends of the ribbon into a little bow. Your homemade sunbonnet is ready to wear.

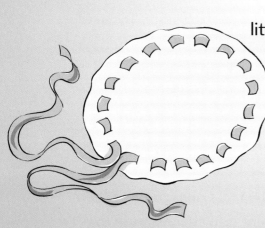

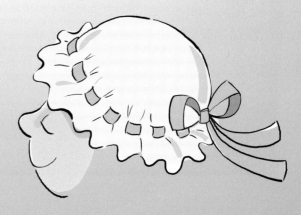

On March 2, 1861, the government created the Nevada Territory, separate from the Utah Territory. Carson City served as the territorial capital. But within weeks, a conflict on the other side of the country—the Civil War (1861–1865)—was to change Nevada's destiny.

War and Statehood

In 1861, the Civil War, a conflict between Northern and Southern states, began. The Northern states were known as the Union (another term used for the United States at that time), and the eleven Southern states that seceded, or withdrew, from the Union were called the Confederacy. Many battles were fought, and more than 600,000 lives were lost during the Civil War. The major battles were fought thousands of miles away, but Nevada played an important role in the war. The Union used Comstock silver to help pay for soldiers and supplies.

Some political leaders in Washington, D.C., wanted to speed Nevada's entry into the Union. As a state, Nevada was likely to support the Union and the Republican Party. Congress passed an enabling act that set up an unusual procedure for Nevada statehood. This act involved the territorial government and the U.S. president but not Congress. On October 31, 1864, Republican president Abraham Lincoln proclaimed Nevada the thirty-sixth state. The new state voted Republican in the U.S. presidential election of 1864, just eight days after achieving statehood. In January 1865, Nevada's new member of the U.S. House of Representatives voted in favor of the Thirteenth Amendment to the U.S. Constitution. When it went into effect later in the year, the Thirteenth Amendment officially abolished (ended) slavery throughout the United States.

Quick Facts

THE BATTLE-BORN STATE
Nevada is sometimes called the Battle-Born State, because it achieved statehood during the Civil War, in 1864. Nevada was not the only state to be admitted to the Union during the Civil War, however. West Virginia became the thirty-fifth U.S. state in 1863.

The transcontinental railroad passed through Nevada. These railroad tracks, under construction in the late 1860s, pass by the Humboldt River near Iron Point.

As the Civil War came to an end in 1865, Nevada continued to grow at a fast pace. The mines of Nevada were now producing silver worth an estimated $23 million every year. In 1869, the first transcontinental railroad, begun in 1863, was completed. The railroad, which passed through Nevada, connected Omaha, Nebraska, and the cities of the East with the fast-growing town of Sacramento, California. A cross-country trip that had once taken six difficult months could now be made in under a week. The railroad helped bring new residents to Nevada. It also helped to establish towns and cities along its route in different parts of Nevada, including Reno and Elko.

People kept coming to the state. Many were Americans from midwestern or eastern states. But by the mid-1870s, nearly half of all Nevadans had been born outside the United States. Among them were Irish miners, German farmers, French-Canadian lumberjacks, Chinese railway workers, and Basque sheepherders (from the Basque region of northern Spain and southern France).

Through the late 1800s, Nevada was very important to the economy of the United States. The country's currency, or money, was based largely on the silver dollar. These dollars were minted from Nevada silver.

Quick Facts

THE FIRST TRAIN ROBBERY

In the early-morning hours of October 5, 1870, five masked men stopped a train outside Reno and rode off with a strongbox containing $50,000 worth of gold and silver. The raid is believed to be the first train robbery in the American West.

Boom and Bust

Nevada's history is like a roller-coaster ride—"boom" times of wealth and prosperity, followed by "busts" that bring hard times. The Comstock boom was followed by the bust of the 1880s, when the U.S. government began to switch the country's currency from silver to gold. Also, the silver in the Carson Valley finally began to run out.

The Nevada economy fell apart, and thousands of people left, in search of work in other parts of the country, such as California. The population of Nevada fell from 62,000 in 1880 to just 47,000 in 1890. Many communities were simply abandoned, to become the ghost towns now scattered across Nevada. Many Nevada ghost towns—such as Rhyolite and Goldfield, west of Las Vegas, and Chloride, near the Hoover Dam—are now tourist attractions.

The boom-and-bust cycle started up again in 1900, when Jim Butler, a rancher in central Nevada, went looking for a stray burro. He discovered a rich vein of silver. Within two years, a town called Tonopah had grown up around the discovery. The town had about three thousand residents. The mines of the Tonopah eventually produced silver valued at $125 million. But when the silver ran out, so did Tonopah's days as "Queen of the Silver Camps."

The Nevada mines that continued to produce were yielding incredible wealth, but most of the people who worked in them remained poor. In 1907, miners in the town of Goldfield, near Tonopah, grew angry over low pay and dangerous working conditions. They went on strike and refused to work in the mines until their lives were improved. The Tonopah-Goldfield strike, the bitterest labor conflict in the state's history, ended only when President Theodore Roosevelt sent in the U.S. Army. The union was broken, and nonunion workers replaced the striking union workers.

Responses to the Great Depression

Nevada was hard hit by an economic downturn called the Great Depression. This economic collapse began in 1929 and caused widespread unemployment and poverty for many years. The federal government tried to create jobs by setting up

FROM RICHES TO GHOSTS

There are hundreds of ghost towns in Nevada—towns that were abandoned when gold or silver deposits ran out and miners left. For example, the population of Belmont (below), in Nye County, peaked at about four thousand in the mid-1870s. Today, it is a historic district with only a few residents.

new agencies, which employed people to carry out various useful projects, such as building roads, bridges, and airports.

One of these building projects, approved by Congress in 1928 but begun in 1931, was a huge dam across the Colorado River. Originally called the Boulder Dam, it was later renamed the Hoover Dam after thirty-first U.S. president Herbert Hoover. The construction of the Hoover Dam took five years, five thousand workers, and more than 7 million tons (6.4 million metric tons) of

By 1935, construction of the Hoover Dam at Black Canyon was nearing completion.

concrete. An entire community, Boulder City, was built to house the workers and their families. The Hoover Dam project helped bring Nevada's economy back to life.

Another decision made in 1931 helped Nevada's economy. Lawmakers in the state decided to make gambling legal, for the first time since 1910. Because gambling was against the law in most of the rest of the country, Nevada's new casinos soon became a popular attraction for out-of-state visitors with money to spend.

Nowhere did the changes have a greater impact than in the sleepy desert town known as Las Vegas, which is Spanish for "the meadows." The first casino in Las Vegas was built in 1931. But the city in those days was nothing like what it is today. Charles Miles, a resident of Las Vegas since 1932, remembered being a five-year-old in the city: "It was a little railroad town at that time—a place where everybody knew everybody and nobody ever locked their doors. It really was a great place to be a kid."

World War II (1939–1945), with its increased demand for metals, helped the Nevada economy rebound. The U.S. government also established several military installations in the state during the war. The well-known Nellis Air Force Base, near Las Vegas, began as the Las Vegas Army Air Field in 1941.

Gaming Takes Hold

Few people saw the money-making potential of Las Vegas until Benjamin "Bugsy" Siegel, a gangster from New York City, opened the Flamingo Hotel and Casino in Las Vegas in 1946. The Flamingo eventually became a huge success, and in the years that followed, more casinos opened in Las Vegas. The greatest stars of the entertainment world in the 1960s—from Frank Sinatra to Elvis Presley— came to Las Vegas to perform. These large-scale shows attracted even more people to the casinos and the gaming tables, bringing more money into Nevada.

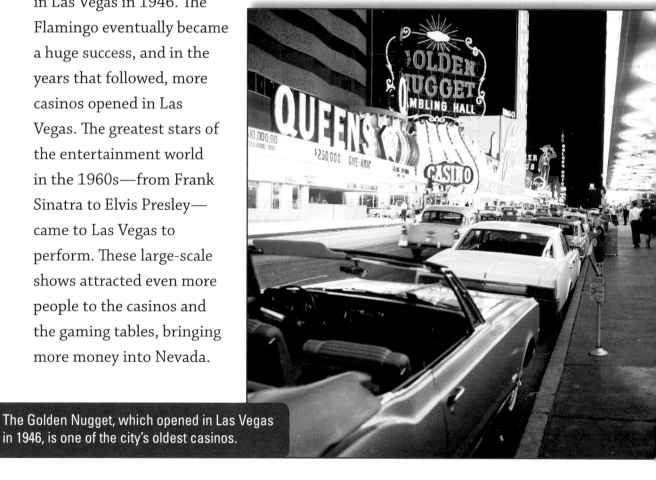

The Golden Nugget, which opened in Las Vegas in 1946, is one of the city's oldest casinos.

Tourism, and a regulated gaming industry, has contributed greatly to Nevada's economy.

Much of the money was going into the wrong pockets, however. Criminal organizations owned or controlled many of the hotels and casinos in Las Vegas. By the late 1950s, the Nevada Gaming Commission was established to license and oversee gambling operations. In the early 1960s, the commission banned people with criminal records from entering or operating a casino, eventually separating crime from the casino operations.

Quick Facts

LAS VEGAS BUFFETS

In the late 1940s, Las Vegas hotel owners were looking for ways to keep customers gambling all night. They came upon the idea of chuck wagons, which were drawn out into the casinos at midnight, offering guests meals for a dollar. Eventually, the chuck wagons changed into inexpensive, all-you-can-eat buffets. Today, these buffets remain a part of the hotel-casino scene, although many are no longer so inexpensive.

The effort to rid Las Vegas of its criminal connections was supported in 1967, when the Nevada legislature passed the Corporate Gaming Act. This law made it possible for corporations to own casinos. In the end, the criminal organizations were unable to raise the enormous amount of money it cost to build new casino-hotels. By the early 1980s, corporations had taken over the running of Las Vegas resorts.

Nevada and Nuclear Testing

In 1951, the U.S. government began to test nuclear bombs in Nevada. The state was chosen because it had large tracts of land with almost no residents. The test area now known as the Nevada Test Site covers about 1,375 square miles (3,560 sq km) of desert. It is bigger than the entire state of Rhode Island. The site is just 65 miles (105 km) northwest of Las Vegas. The U.S. government conducted hundreds of its nuclear weapons tests here.

In the early days, most Americans believed nuclear testing was necessary for the country's security. The Union of Soviet Socialist Republics (USSR) and other countries were developing nuclear weapons, and the United States wanted to be able to deter international war or defend itself during a nuclear attack.

A dry lake bed called Frenchman Flat at the Nevada Test Site was the location for several underground nuclear tests in the late 1960s.

But many people were not aware of the long-term effects of radiation, which is given off during weapons tests. Radiation can cause many serious health problems, including cancer.

Nevadans worry about the long-term impact of all those nuclear explosions on the environment and on their health. A great deal of radiation from the Nevada Test Site passed into the state's air, water, and soil. Many people point to high rates of serious illness—especially in the area downwind from the site—as the direct result of the nuclear radiation.

Modern Nevada

Nevadans still worry about their environment. Hundreds of thousands of people have poured into the state in the past half-century, seeking the good life that Nevada promised them and their families. And as they have arrived, they have changed the state and its environment.

The fast-growing population of Nevada required new housing, new roads, and new schools. Until the economic downturn that began in late 2007, many parts of the state were booming with construction. This was especially true in the area around Las Vegas, which was expanding several miles farther out into the desert every year, as new housing developments were built. By 2011, however, average home prices in Nevada had fallen by 65 percent, and the state's unemployment rate had risen by more than 7 percentage points. It was one of the U.S. states hardest hit by the economic slump and housing bust.

Nevada has experienced many booms and busts, and there were indications by 2012 that the economy was improving again. The state has always managed to protect its special way of life. Most Nevadans are confident that it will continue to be able to do so.

★ **10,000** BCE The earliest American Indians, known as Paleo-Indians, live in what is now Nevada.

★ **300** CE–**1150** CE The Ancestral Puebloans create a civilization in the Southwest, then mysteriously disappear.

★ **1776** Francisco Garcés is probably the first European to pass through the region that includes Nevada.

★ **1827** Jedediah Smith leads a party across the land that includes present-day Nevada.

★ **1843–1844** John Charles Frémont explores the region.

★ **1848** Mexico signs the Treaty of Guadalupe Hidalgo, granting the United States a vast area of the Southwest that includes present-day Nevada.

★ **1850** The U.S. Congress creates the Utah Territory, which includes most of modern-day Nevada.

★ **1851** Mormon Station, near present-day Carson City, becomes the area's first permanent white settlement.

★ **1859** Gold and silver are discovered in Nevada's Comstock Lode.

★ **1860** The Paiute are defeated in the Pyramid Lake War.

★ **1861** The U.S. Congress creates the Nevada Territory.

★ **1864** Nevada becomes the thirty-sixth U.S. state.

★ **1900** Silver is discovered at Tonopah, beginning a new mining boom.

★ **1914** Women gain the right to vote in Nevada.

★ **1936** The Boulder Dam, renamed the Hoover Dam in 1947, is completed.

★ **1946** The Flamingo Hotel and Casino opens, starting the modern era of Las Vegas development.

★ **1951** The U.S. government begins testing nuclear weapons in the southern Nevada desert.

★ **1967** Nevada's state legislature passes the Corporate Gaming Act, which permits corporations to own casinos.

★ **2007** Nevadan Harry Reid becomes majority leader of the U.S. Senate.

★ **2010** Nevada's population reaches more than 2.7 million.

The People

For decades, Nevada has been one of the fastest-growing states in the country. In 1980, its population was about 800,000. By 2010, that number had increased to more than 2.7 million. Nevada's population more than tripled in just three decades. Most of the state's new residents have settled in Clark County, the area that includes Las Vegas. The explosive growth in Nevada's population makes clear that many people are drawn to this land, and to the spirit of these people. The new Nevadans have changed the Silver State in many ways, making it a more diverse place.

Hispanic Americans

Hispanic Americans have a long history in Nevada, which was part of Mexico before 1848. Mexican Americans were present when Las Vegas was founded in 1905. For many years, Hispanics were a small minority in Nevada. In recent years, however, Hispanic Americans have made up the fastest-growing segment of Nevada's population. The number of Hispanic residents grew from about 394,000 in 2000 to more than 716,000 in 2010. This represents an increase of almost 82 percent. More than one-quarter of Nevada's population is of Hispanic ancestry.

Most Hispanic Americans in Nevada trace their origins to Mexico. But as this group has increased in size, its diversity has increased as well. Today, the

A young Nevadan at a rodeo guides her horse around a pole.

state's Hispanic-American population includes residents of Puerto Rican or Cuban ancestry, as well as many people who trace their origins to Central America or South America.

The Earliest Nevadans

American Indians, who have been in the area for thousands of years, were the earliest Nevadans. They experienced a long, tragic decline after the arrival of white people. They were often forced off the land their ancestors had lived on for centuries. They are now one of the smallest—and poorest—minority groups in the state.

American Indians make up slightly more than one percent of Nevada's population. Many of them still live on reservations, such as the Duck Valley Indian Reservation, which covers almost 300,000 acres (120,000 ha) on the Nevada-Idaho border and is home to more than 1,700 Paiute and Shoshone.

In recent years, Nevada's American Indians have successfully argued court cases to take back land they believe was unfairly taken from them—or at least

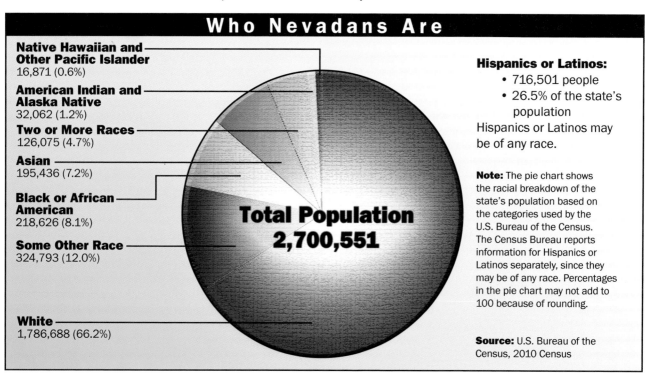

Who Nevadans Are

Native Hawaiian and Other Pacific Islander
16,871 (0.6%)

American Indian and Alaska Native
32,062 (1.2%)

Two or More Races
126,075 (4.7%)

Asian
195,436 (7.2%)

Black or African American
218,626 (8.1%)

Some Other Race
324,793 (12.0%)

White
1,786,688 (66.2%)

Total Population 2,700,551

Hispanics or Latinos:
- 716,501 people
- 26.5% of the state's population

Hispanics or Latinos may be of any race.

Note: The pie chart shows the racial breakdown of the state's population based on the categories used by the U.S. Bureau of the Census. The Census Bureau reports information for Hispanics or Latinos separately, since they may be of any race. Percentages in the pie chart may not add to 100 because of rounding.

Source: U.S. Bureau of the Census, 2010 Census

Paiute Indians gather to celebrate their traditions at an annual powwow in Las Vegas.

receive payment for that land. In 1970, a federal court awarded the Southern Paiute millions of dollars to settle one of these court actions. The American Indians of Nevada have used settlement payments to build new businesses that bring in money and create jobs. One of these businesses is the Las Vegas Paiute Golf Resort, which boasts three championship golf courses. Other groups own cattle ranches and mining operations. Perhaps most important, these groups have worked hard to keep their traditional cultures alive, through museums and festivals such as powwows, which are traditional American Indian gatherings that include music, dancing, and storytelling.

African Americans

African Americans, too, have a long history in Nevada. In 1850, James Pierson Beckwourth, a mountain man born into slavery in Virginia, discovered an important route for wagon trains through the Sierra Nevada to California. This path is known as the Beckwourth Trail. Benjamin Palmer, another former slave, is believed to have been the first African-American settler in Nevada. He built a 400-acre (160-ha) ranch near Sheridan in 1853, and he worked it for more than forty years. Today, African Americans make up more than 8 percent of the Silver State's population.

The Basques

The Basques are a prominent ethnic group in Nevada. Most Basque Nevadans have ancestors who came to the state from Spain. Many Basques saw a resemblance between northern Nevada and their homes in the Pyrenees Mountains region, on the border between Spain and France. When they arrived, many settled in the northern part of the state around Reno, Elko, and Winnemucca. Many took up their traditional occupations, becoming sheepherders and, eventually, successful sheep ranchers.

Quick Facts

SPANISH RANCH FOUNDER
In 1873, a Basque immigrant named Pedro Altube founded the Spanish Ranch, a huge cattle operation in the Independence Valley. He brought so many of his friends and relatives to America that he is known as the Father of the Basques in the West.

RECIPE FOR BASQUE GARLIC AND BREAD SOUP

This traditional Basque recipe turns bread into a delicious, hearty soup. It is simple to make.

WHAT YOU NEED

$^1/_2$ cup (120 milliliters) olive oil

6 garlic cloves, peeled and sliced thin

$^1/_2$ slightly dry French baguette bread, cut into thin slices

Paprika

4 cups (1 liter) water or chicken broth

Salt

Pepper

6 large eggs

Have an adult help you heat the olive oil in a heavy pot or skillet over medium heat. Add the garlic and stir it for 2 to 3 minutes with a wooden spoon. The garlic should become a rich golden color. Be careful not to burn the mixture.

Add the sliced bread, and turn the slices several times so that they absorb the oil. Sprinkle some paprika over the bread and mix it well.

Add the water or broth, and cook for 10 to 15 minutes. Continue to stir it until the soup is heated through. The bread should soak up a lot of the liquid.

You can add some salt or pepper to the soup if you like.

Once the soup is heated, have an adult help you crack the eggs, and slide them onto the surface of the soup. Be sure not to break the yolks. Cook the soup for at least another 5 minutes so that the eggs are fully cooked. The yolks should be firm, not runny, and you should not be able to see through the whites of the eggs.

Spoon the soup gently into shallow bowls, allowing one egg per serving. Dig in and enjoy.

Modern Basques in Nevada have also built many hotels. One of the great pleasures of a drive across Nevada today is stopping at a small-town hotel for a Basque meal. This meal could include traditional foods such as the spiced-pork sausage called chorizo, garbanzo beans, and grilled lamb.

The Basque culture is very old and distinct, and the Basque language is believed to be unrelated to any other language in the world. Like other cultural groups, the state's Basques have their own traditions and festivals, such as the annual National Basque Festival in Elko.

Nevada's Basque people honor their heritage with festivals that include dancing, food, and other traditional activities.

Every January or February, Las Vegas celebrates the Chinese New Year with a dragon and lion dance.

Asian Americans

Many people of Asian origin or descent have also come to Nevada. Some are Asian Americans who have moved from other states. Others are recent immigrants from such countries as India, China, Japan, and the Philippines. Some Asian Nevadans are descendants of the Chinese who came to the region more than one hundred years ago. Most of those early immigrants came to work on the transcontinental and other railroads. They faced terrible discrimination. As with many immigrants, it was very difficult for the early Chinese residents to own land and run businesses. Today, however, many Asian Americans have thriving businesses and host various cultural festivals.

Sarah Winnemucca Hopkins: American Indian Activist and Writer

Sarah Winnemucca Hopkins was the daughter of a Northern Paiute chief. Born in 1844, she spent many years working to protect American Indian rights. Hopkins gave lectures and met with political leaders to raise awareness of the mistreatment of American Indians. Her 1883 autobiography, *Life Among the Paiutes: Their Wrongs and Claims*, is thought to be the first book ever published by an American Indian woman. Hopkins died in 1891.

Wovoka

Wovoka, also known as Jack Wilson, was a Paiute Indian born around 1856. In the late 1880s, he spoke of a new age in which whites would disappear and American Indians would live in a world of plenty, as long as they behaved justly and performed a sacred dance. Wovoka's teachings, which grew into the Ghost Dance Movement, helped inspire a protest among the Lakota Sioux at Wounded Knee, South Dakota, in 1890, but the uprising ended in tragedy. The U.S. cavalry killed almost two hundred men, women, and children. Wovoka's message was abandoned. He died in 1932.

James Casey: Businessman

James Casey, born in Nevada in 1888, moved as a child to Seattle, Washington. After his father died, he worked as a delivery boy to help support his family. By age nineteen, Casey had cofounded the American Messenger Company, which in time became the giant United Parcel Service (UPS). He also set up the Annie E. Casey Foundation in honor of his mother to help disadvantaged children. Casey died in 1983.

Anne Martin: Activist

Born in Empire in 1875, Anne Martin taught at Nevada State University and became involved in the women's suffrage movement. Partly as a result of Martin's efforts, Nevada's women received the right to vote in 1914—six years before an amendment to the U.S. Constitution gave women the right to vote nationwide. Martin ran as an independent for the U.S. Senate twice, in 1918 and 1920. After World War I (1914–1918), she worked for world peace. Martin died in 1951.

Steve Wynn: Resort Developer

Steve Wynn was born in New Haven, Connecticut, in 1942. After the sudden death of his father in 1963, Wynn left college to take over the family business—a bingo operation in Maryland. He moved to Las Vegas in 1967 and never looked back. His vision for world-class casino-hotels led to a revitalization of the Las Vegas Strip in the 1990s. In 1998, Wynn opened a $1.6 billion luxury resort, featuring an artificial lake and a museum-quality art collection.

Andre Agassi: Tennis Player

Andre Agassi, born in Las Vegas in 1970, learned to play tennis from his Armenian immigrant father. As one of the world's top players, Agassi won all four Grand Slam events—Wimbledon and the Australian, French, and U.S. opens—as well as an Olympic gold medal (at the 1996 Summer Games in Atlanta, Georgia). In 2001, Agassi married fellow tennis great Steffi Graf. His charitable foundation, established in 1994, supports at-risk children. In 2011, Agassi was inducted into the International Tennis Hall of Fame.

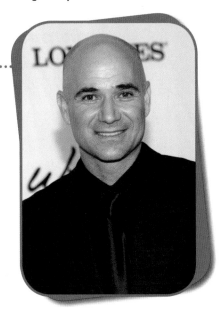

Families from around the world make Nevada their home.

A Place of Opportunities

Most people who have moved to Nevada from different states or countries came to Nevada to work, and work hard. They also came for Nevada's special way of life. Many were drawn to the fast-paced life of Las Vegas. Others liked the slower pace of the state's small towns and suburban areas.

Many of the people who come to live in Nevada today are retired. Nevada has one of the largest retired populations in the United States. Retirees from all over the country come to Nevada because of the many exciting recreational activities, the low cost of living, and, of course, the warm, sunny weather. Many live in retirement communities.

The many changes in Nevada in recent years have made it a fascinating and complicated place. The modern world is very closely linked to the natural environment. Even the glittering hotels and casinos of Las Vegas and Reno are just a few minutes away from the natural beauty of the desert and the mountains. Many Nevadans, in fact, barely notice the neon-lit attractions that draw tourists. Some prefer hiking in the desert, visiting a museum, or enjoying local festivals.

In many ways, the people of Nevada have the best of all worlds. They treasure their pioneer heritage and the untouched beauty of the wilderness. At the same time, they are proud of the rapid pace of progress in the Silver State. Most Nevadans share great confidence in their state and hope that its future will be as exciting as its past.

Nevadans appreciate the many cultural opportunities in their state, including Lied Discovery Children's Museum in Las Vegas.

★ National Cowboy Poetry Gathering

Every year, at the end of January, the town of Elko, in the heart of cowboy country, celebrates its Old West heritage. That means big hats, big boots, big stories (some folks might even call them tall tales), and, of course, poetry.

★ Jim Butler Days

Once a year—every Memorial Day weekend, at the end of May—Tonopah remembers the man who went looking for a lost burro and started the last great Nevada mining rush. Activities include a parade and a street dance. Also featured are contests of old-time mining skills, such as timber tossing and spike driving.

★ National Basque Festival

The Basques of Nevada say "*Ongi etorri*" ("Welcome") at this grand celebration of their traditional culture, every July in Elko. The high point is the "running from the bulls," when lots of people let themselves be chased through the streets by live bulls.

★ Spirit of Wovoka Days

Every August, the town of Yerington, on the Walker River, celebrates the legacy of Wovoka, the Paiute mystic and founder of the Ghost Dance Movement. Among the highlights of this powwow are traditional shawl and bustle dances by various American Indian groups.

★ Great Reno Balloon Race

Early September finds the blue skies above Reno filled with hot air balloons, for the Great Reno Balloon Race. More than a hundred balloons participate in this three-day event. An average of 150,000 people come to enjoy the beautiful spectacle.

★ Virginia City Camel Races

This annual event, held in Virginia City in September, looks back at a time when camels carried freight to and from the mines of the Comstock Lode. In addition to camels, ostriches and emus are featured. The event takes place at the top of a historic mining quarry, combining entertainment with gold-rush-era nostalgia.

★ National Championship Air Races and Air Show

Every September, the skies above Reno roar with the sounds of different kinds of aircraft, from World War II fighters to racing jets. There are five days of racing action and six classes of aircraft, with speeds exceeding 500 miles (800 km) per hour.

★ Hispanic International Day Parade and Festival

On the second Saturday of every October, the city of Henderson hosts this family-oriented cultural parade followed by a music festival. The local Hispanic community shares new and traditional music, food, and art from various countries.

★ Nevada Day Celebration

Carson City celebrates the day Nevada became a state—October 31, 1864—with a parade and other festivities. Many of the events, such as the World Championship Rock Drilling Contest, recall the Silver State's mining past.

★ National Finals Rodeo

For one week in December, Las Vegas becomes the Cowboy Capital of the World. This annual event—with bareback riding, calf roping, and barrel racing—is the most important competition on the rodeo circuit.

How the Government Works

The people of Nevada are represented by three different levels of government: local, state, and federal. Each of these levels is, in its own way, extremely important to the running of the state.

The state's cities, towns, and villages all have their own local governments. Most have mayors and city or town councils, elected by local voters every two years. Mayors and councils make decisions about property taxes, schools, and other local issues. Nevada is also divided into seventeen counties, managed by boards of commissioners that are elected every two years. One example of a county government's responsibilities is maintaining police departments.

Nevada's American Indian reservations have their own governments. The residents choose their leaders, who are responsible for police and fire departments, road repairs, and other important services within the reservations.

Nevada's state government, which makes decisions that affect the entire state, is based on a system of checks and balances. This means that the three separate branches, or parts, of the state government—the executive, legislative, and judicial branches—work together and no branch can become too powerful.

How a Bill Becomes a Law

The governor, local government officials, organizations, and citizens often ask the members of the Nevada state assembly and senate to pass new laws or change

The Nevada state capitol, built in 1871, is located in Carson City.

Branches of Government

EXECUTIVE ★ ★ ★ ★ ★ ★ ★ ★

The executive branch, headed by the governor, handles the day-to-day management of the state and makes sure that Nevada's laws and regulations are properly enforced. The governor and the other senior officials of the executive branch—the lieutenant governor, secretary of state, attorney general, treasurer, and controller—are elected by the state's voters. These officials serve four-year terms and cannot hold office for more than two terms.

LEGISLATIVE ★ ★ ★ ★ ★ ★ ★ ★

The legislative branch creates new state laws and makes changes to existing laws. The Nevada legislature has two chambers, or houses: the forty-two-member assembly and the twenty-one-member senate. Members of the assembly serve two-year terms, while members of the senate serve for four years. Both are elected by the voters of their individual state electoral districts. Legislators may not seek election to a house in which they have served twelve years or more.

JUDICIAL ★ ★ ★ ★ ★ ★ ★ ★ ★

The judicial branch—the court system—makes sure that Nevada's laws are properly interpreted and enforced. The highest level of the judicial branch, the state supreme court, hears appeals from the lower courts and decides whether new laws agree with Nevada's constitution. The supreme court has a chief justice and six associate justices, who are elected for six-year terms. Sixty district court justices, who also serve six-year terms, hear important criminal and civil cases. Sixty-four justices sit in the justice courts, which preside over the preliminary phases of important criminal and civil cases. Municipal courts handle less serious cases. The district courts also act as appeal courts for cases from justice and municipal courts.

existing ones. When a lawmaker agrees with a suggestion, he or she proposes a new law—called a bill—and a legislative attorney prepares a draft version of the bill.

Then a committee from the house where the bill has arisen considers the draft bill. Most of these committees have a special focus, such as education, taxes, or agriculture. Committee members discuss the details of the bill. They usually make changes, called amendments. If they support the bill, they present it to the house, which debates and then votes on it.

If the house where the bill originates approves, or passes, the draft bill, it goes to the other house, where the process begins again. If each house passes a different version of the bill, the bill is sent to a joint conference committee. This committee, which includes representatives from both houses, tries to create a compromise version of the bill. This new bill is then presented to both houses for a vote. It must be passed by the house of origin first.

To become law, a bill must be approved in a vote by a majority of the members of both houses. This requires twenty-two votes in the assembly and eleven votes in the senate. Bills with tax or fee increases require a two-thirds majority in each house to pass. Once the bill has been approved, it is sent to the governor, who either

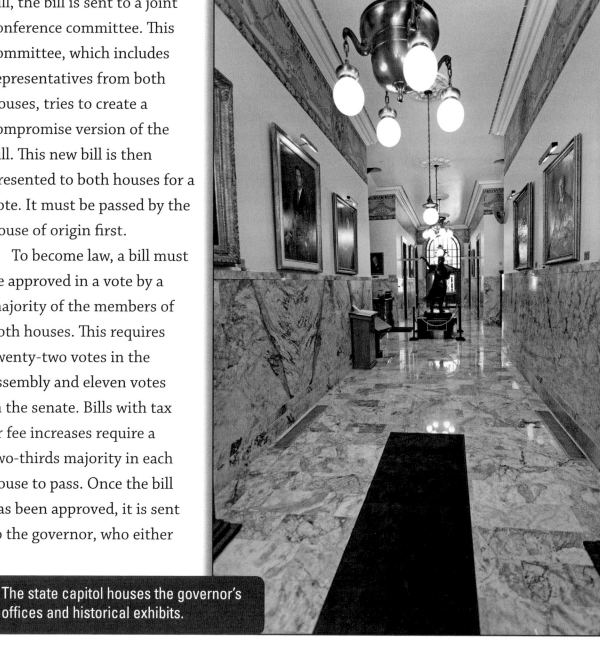

The state capitol houses the governor's offices and historical exhibits.

LAWS ARISING DIRECTLY FROM CITIZENS

Nevadans can also create laws directly, using the initiative process. If enough people sign a petition in favor of doing so, a proposed law—an initiative—is placed on the ballot during statewide elections. If a majority of voters approve the measure in two different elections, then it becomes law without going through the legislature.

signs it, making it a law, or vetoes—rejects—it. The legislature can override the governor's veto, by giving the bill a two-thirds majority vote in each house. If that happens, the bill becomes law even though the governor rejected it.

The Federal Government in Nevada

Nevada is also represented in the U.S. Congress in Washington, D.C. The state's voters elect two senators, like all U.S. states, and four members of the House of Representatives. (Nevada gained a fourth representative, as of 2013, because of its large population increase, as recorded in the 2010 Census.)

The Nevada State Library and Archives, located in Carson City, supports Nevada democracy by providing information services to local and state government, libraries, businesses, and citizens.

U.S. SENATOR FROM NEVADA

Harry Reid was born in 1939 in Searchlight, Nevada, where he still lives. He has served as U.S. senator for the state since 1987. In 2007, Reid became the majority leader of the U.S. Senate. Over the years, he has developed a reputation as a skillful legislator and a consensus builder.

Representation at the federal level is especially important in Nevada, because the federal government is unusually powerful in the state.

The U.S. government owns or controls more than 87 percent of the land in Nevada, in the form of military bases, national parks, and other holdings. There is sometimes conflict between Nevadans and the federal government. A rancher who wants to herd cattle on a particular piece of land may have to deal with many different federal agencies, such as the Bureau of Land Management, the Fish and Wildlife Service, the Forest Service, and even the military.

One type of government activity probably troubles many Nevadans more than any other: the past use of the desert as a place to test nuclear weapons and its potential future use as a site to store nuclear waste materials. Nevadans' nuclear concerns became even more serious in 1987, when the federal government announced plans to create a huge storage area for nuclear waste at Yucca Mountain, at the edge of the Nevada Test Site. The plan called for 77,000 tons

Environmental activist Bob Fulkerson leads a rally in Reno against the proposed Yucca Mountain nuclear waste project.

(70,000 t) of radioactive material—such as spent fuel from nuclear power plants—to be stored at Yucca Mountain.

Despite years of government assurances that Yucca Mountain would be safe, a majority of Nevadans—more than 70 percent, according to some opinion polls—opposed the plan. Although a plan to go ahead with the Yucca Mountain project had been approved earlier, President Barack Obama halted work on the project in 2009. In 2010, he appointed the Blue Ribbon Commission on America's Nuclear Future to recommend a long-term solution to disposing of nuclear waste in the United States. In 2012, the commission released its recommendations. The first of these was that a consent-based approach should be used to select sites for nuclear waste facilities. The commission simply said that if the local people opposed a project, it would not succeed. The statement was a victory for Nevadans who had opposed the Yucca Mountain project. However, the actual location of a nuclear waste storage facility remained to be determined.

Making a Difference

If there is an issue you care about, you should get involved. The best way to start is by learning as much as you can about the issue. You can read your local newspaper, follow the news on television, the radio, or the Internet, and talk to parents and teachers.

Your next step should be to contact your representatives in the local, state, or federal government—or all three—to make sure your voice is heard. You can do this by telephone, letter, or e-mail, or even in person.

When the state legislature is in session, you can watch debates and sit in on committee meetings. Nevada state legislators officially convene, or meet, every two years. You can also make an appointment to visit your representatives at their offices.

Contacting Lawmakers

★ ★ ★ ★ ★ ★ ★ ★ ★ ★ ★ ★

All citizens can contact the government officials who represent them to express their views about proposed legislation and other issues.
To contact the governor, go to

http://gov.nv.gov

Click on Contact on the menu bar. Then click on the link Email the Governor to send the governor an e-mail message.
To contact your state legislators, go to

http://www.leg.state.nv.us

To find your assembly member, click on Assembly and then Contact List and Email. For your state senator, click on Senate and then Contact List and Email.
To contact your representatives in the U.S. Congress, go to

http://www.congress.org

Then enter your zip code.

Making a Living

The people of Nevada make their living in many different ways, both old and new. A typical Nevada worker might be a hotel desk clerk in Lake Tahoe, a cowboy on a ranch outside Elko, or a teacher, shop owner, or nurse in any community in the state. Nevada's economy needs all these types of workers—and many more.

From the Land

Despite the changes the past few decades have brought, Nevada has not left behind all its traditional ways of making a living. Mining is still an important industry. Open-pit and underground mines use advanced technologies to find precious metals such as gold and silver, semiprecious stones such as turquoise and opals, and construction materials, including gypsum, limestone, and clays. The Ruth Copper Pit, located near Ely, is said to be one of the largest open-pit mines in the world.

Today's mining is not the same backbreaking work it was in the 1800s. Satellite images help locate mineral deposits. The use of remotely controlled digging equipment means that miners do not have to go into dangerous underground areas. But this modern technology means that Nevada's mines do not need as many workers as they used to. Less than one percent of Nevada workers are now employed in the mining industry.

For many Nevadans, enjoying their leisure time is as important as earning a living. This hiker backpacks on the Tahoe Rim Trail overlooking Lake Tahoe.

Workers & Industries

Industry	Number of People Working in That Industry	Percentage of All Workers Who Are Working in That Industry
Publishing, media, entertainment, hotels, and restaurants	329,442	27.5%
Education and health care	185,466	15.5%
Wholesale and retail businesses	166,257	13.9%
Professionals, scientists, and managers	125,940	10.5%
Construction	75,833	6.3%
Banking and finance, insurance, and real estate	73,250	6.1%
Government	60,932	5.1%
Transportation and public utilities	55,698	4.7%
Other services	55,265	4.6%
Manufacturing	49,035	4.1%
Farming, fishing, forestry, and mining	19,776	1.7%
Totals	1,196,894	100%

Notes: Figures above do not include people in the armed forces.
"Professionals" includes people such as doctors and lawyers.

Source: U.S. Bureau of the Census, 2010 estimates

Agriculture has always been difficult in Nevada and now represents a very small part of the state's economy. Cattle and sheep ranches are the main source of agricultural income. The meat and wool they produce are shipped all over the world. Horse ranches and dairy and poultry farms have become important in western and southeastern Nevada.

Nevada's farms grow food crops, such as potatoes and onions, and livestock feed, such as barley and hay. Alfalfa is a leading crop in the state, and alfalfa hay is sold to dairy farms in surrounding states. Alfalfa cubes and compressed bales are also exported overseas. Alfalfa seeds are another substantial crop.

In places where irrigation and conservation projects ensure an abundant supply of water, farmers can even grow crops that would not ordinarily grow in such a dry climate, such as tomatoes and grapes. Farmers and ranchers sell many of the

GOLD MINING TODAY
Nevada leads the nation in the production of gold. It is the most commercially valuable of all Nevada's minerals. Gold mining in Nevada is centered in the Elko region.

A boy on horseback helps move cattle to a new pasture in Baker.

IRRIGATION FOR MORE THAN A CENTURY

The Newlands Project—the first irrigation project ever built by the U.S. government—diverted the waters of the Carson and Truckee rivers to the Lahontan Valley. The 1903 to 1908 project brought water, and farming, to an 87,000-acre (35,000-ha) stretch of desert through a long series of canals, dams, and irrigation ditches. The project continues to operate today.

state's agricultural products locally but also export products to other states and countries. Although agriculture is a small part of the state's economy, it is still worth more than $500 million every year.

Other Industries

Other industries continue to grow in Nevada. Manufacturing is becoming a more important segment of the state's economy, especially in Reno, Henderson, and North Las Vegas.

Nevada's central position in the western United States makes it an important transportation hub. Both Las Vegas and Reno have international airports. Two freight railroads cross Nevada, and Amtrak passenger service connects Nevada to other states. Reno, Las Vegas, and the Elko/Ely region are Nevada's three most important transportation centers. Trucking and warehousing are flourishing in Nevada in part due to its geographic location. In addition, the state does not tax goods that are continuing in transit, making Nevada an appealing site for international business.

New businesses that open up in Nevada are attracted by the state's skilled workers, low costs, and—perhaps most important—low taxes. Nevadans pay less tax than the residents of almost any other state. They pay no state taxes on earnings from their jobs, on the profits their businesses make, or on money they inherit from their families.

More than 50 percent of Nevada's workers are employed in service industries. Anyone whose job involves doing something for someone else instead of making a product is a service worker. Doctors and lawyers, teachers and college professors, real estate agents and electricians are all service workers. So are the many people who work in the hotels, restaurants, casinos, and resorts that serve the millions of tourists visiting the state each year.

Nevada provides a number of educational opportunities for its citizens. The University of Nevada is located in Reno. The University of Nevada, Las Vegas (UNLV) began as a branch of the University of Nevada but is now an independent institution. Elko, Carson City, Reno, Douglas, Fallon, and North Las Vegas all have two-year colleges. The University of Southern Nevada and Great Basin College also serve many Nevadans.

More than 20,000 undergraduate students attend the University of Nevada, Las Vegas (UNLV).

Gold

Nevada's early economy was built on silver mining, but today, gold is an even more important resource. The state is the third-richest source of gold in the world, after South Africa and Australia.

Manufacturing

Nevada's manufacturing sector is concentrated mostly around Reno and the Las Vegas suburbs of Henderson and North Las Vegas. Nevada's manufacturers produce industrial machinery, computer software, food products, chemicals, and printing products. The world's largest producer of casino gaming equipment is located in Reno.

Tourism

Tourism is by far Nevada's most important industry. Outdoor activities are popular attractions. The cities are, too—Las Vegas alone welcomed more than 37 million visitors in 2010. These visitors spent almost $37 billion at the city's hotels, casinos, and other attractions.

Turquoise

Nevada has been a major producer of turquoise since the 1930s. Turquoise was a valuable trade item for the American Indians of the Southwest, who now use it in handmade jewelry that collectors all over the world prize.

Transportation

A superb road, rail, and air transportation system keeps people and goods moving in and out of Nevada. Las Vegas's McCarran International Airport handles more than 40 million passengers every year, which makes it the tenth-busiest in the world.

Water

No natural resource is more important to Nevada than water. Even though it is the driest state in the country, Nevada actually sends water to other places. Lake Mead, formed by the Hoover Dam, provides water to millions of Nevadans and Californians. Huge turbines at the Hoover Dam also turn the power of rushing water into electricity. In fact, electricity from the Hoover Dam travels along transmission lines to Los Angeles.

Tourism

The most important sector of Nevada's economy is tourism. This industry brings in more than half of the state's income, just as it has for more than half a century. While many parts of Nevada are ideal for tourists, Las Vegas tends to be the most popular. The city has the ten largest hotels in the United States—and more hotel rooms than anywhere else in the world.

Many of the hotels and resorts in Las Vegas are inspired by certain themes. Some are designed to resemble cities in different countries. One is a replica of an ancient Egyptian pyramid, while others look like nineteenth-century Paris or a tropical island. Most of the hotels in Las Vegas have casinos and other gambling opportunities. Nevada—and Las Vegas especially—has become an ideal spot for conferences and conventions. With the large choices in hotels and resorts, many business groups and other organizations choose to hold their conventions in the state.

Over the past few decades, the state has become a great place for family vacations. There are many shows, concerts, and other forms of entertainment

The Luxor Hotel, which opened in Las Vegas in 1993, is named after the Egyptian city.

The National Association for Stock Car Auto Racing (NASCAR) Sprint Cup series takes to the track at the Las Vegas Motor Speedway.

for the whole family to enjoy. Nevada has many resorts, spas, and golf courses that offer a fun, relaxing time.

Although Nevada has no professional sports teams, a wealth of spectator sports entertains both residents and visitors. The University of Nevada and UNLV have a number of popular sports teams. UNLV won the National Collegiate Athletic Association (NCAA) Men's Division I Basketball Championship in 1990. Major golf tournaments and the National Finals Rodeo are held in Las Vegas. Auto racing enthusiasts go to Las Vegas Motor Speedway to enjoy National Association for Stock Car Auto Racing (NASCAR) events.

Tourism in Nevada extends beyond sports and entertainment. Many visitors go to Virginia City and other places that preserve memories of the days of

Tourists can visit a real Nevada ghost town in Goldfield.

pioneers and silver miners. Other tourists are drawn to the natural beauty of wild Nevada. They backpack in the Sierra Nevada, water-ski on Lake Mead, or view ancient bristlecone pines in Great Basin National Park.

Workers are probably Nevada's most important resource. Their determination, drive, and energy show the same spirit as in the state's early days. While modern Nevadans are more likely to work for a resort hotel or a software company than a silver mine or a cattle ranch, they continue to show a pioneering spirit. The people of Nevada are the main reason so many visitors come to the Silver State—and will keep coming for many years.

Hikers travel up a boulder slope in Nevada's Great Basin National Park.

The Nevada state flag, adopted in 1929 and revised in 1991,
has a cobalt-blue background. In the upper left-hand corner is
a five-pointed silver star with the word Nevada in gold below it.
Above the star is a gold scroll with the words Battle Born. To the
right and left of the star are sprays of sagebrush.

Nevada's state seal, officially adopted in 1866, shows the words
The Great Seal of the State of Nevada in a circle on a cobalt-blue field.
Inside the circle is a picture of farm equipment, a mine, and a steam train,
with the sun rising above mountains in the background. A scroll beneath
the picture bears Nevada's state motto "All for Our Country."
Thirty-six stars on the inner circle of the seal represent Nevada
as the thirty-sixth state to join the Union.

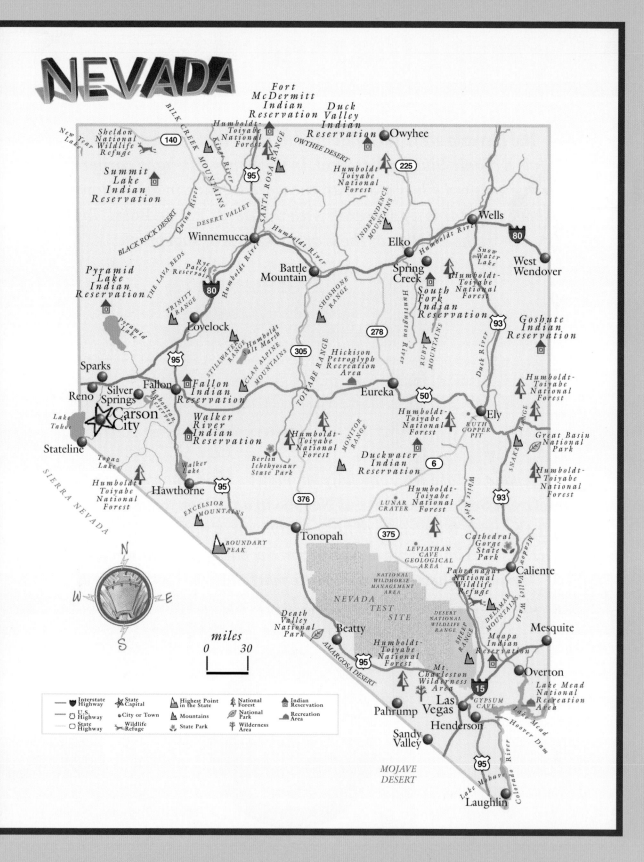

NEVADA

Fort McDermitt Indian Reservation

Duck Valley Indian Reservation

140

Sheldon National Wildlife Refuge

New Year Lake

Humboldt-Toiyabe National Forest

BILK CREEK MOUNTAINS

Kings River

OWYHEE DESERT

Owyhee

225

Summit Lake Indian Reservation

Quinn River

DESERT VALLEY

SANTA ROSA RANGE

95

Humboldt River

Humboldt-Toiyabe National Forest

INDEPENDENCE MOUNTAINS

Wells

80

BLACK ROCK DESERT

Winnemucca

Humboldt River

Elko

Spring Creek

Snow Water Lake

West Wendover

Pyramid Lake Indian Reservation

THE LAVA BEDS

Rye Patch Reservoir

80

Battle Mountain

SHOSHONE RANGE

South Fork Indian Reservation

Humboldt-Toiyabe National Forest

Goshute Indian Reservation

TRINITY RANGE

Pyramid Lake

Lovelock

STILLWATER RANGE

Humboldt Salt Marsh

CLAN ALPINE MOUNTAINS

305

TOIYABE RANGE

278

Hickison Petroglyph Recreation Area

Duck River

93

Sparks

95

Fallon

Fallon Indian Reservation

Walker River Indian Reservation

Eureka

50

Ely

Humboldt-Toiyabe National Forest

Silver Springs

Reno

Lake Tahoe

Carson City

RUBY MOUNTAINS

Humboldt-Toiyabe National Forest

RUTH COPPER PIT

Great Basin National Park

Stateline

Topaz Lake

Walker Lake

Berlin Ichthyosaur State Park

MONITOR RANGE

Duckwater Indian Reservation

6

SNAKE RANGE

Humboldt-Toiyabe National Forest

SIERRA NEVADA

Humboldt-Toiyabe National Forest

Hawthorne

95

EXCELSIOR MOUNTAINS

376

Humboldt-Toiyabe National Forest

White River

LUNAR CRATER

93

BOUNDARY PEAK

Tonopah

375

LEVIATHAN CAVE GEOLOGICAL AREA

Cathedral Gorge State Park

Caliente

N / E / W / S

miles
0   30

NATIONAL WILDHORSE MANAGEMENT AREA

NEVADA TEST SITE

DESERT NATIONAL WILDLIFE RANGE

Pahranagat National Wildlife Refuge

DELMAR MOUNTAINS

Meadow Valley Wash

Death Valley National Park

Beatty

95

AMARGOSA DESERT

Humboldt-Toiyabe National Forest

SHEEP RANGE

Mt. Charleston Wilderness Area

Moapa Indian Reservation

Mesquite

Overton

15

Lake Mead National Recreation Area

Pahrump

Las Vegas

Henderson

GYPSUM CAVE

Sandy Valley

95

Lake Mead

Hoover Dam

MOJAVE DESERT

Colorado River

Lake Mohave

Laughlin

Legend

- Interstate Highway
- State Capital
- Highest Point in the State
- National Forest
- Indian Reservation
- U.S. Highway
- City or Town
- Mountains
- National Park
- Recreation Area
- State Highway
- Wildlife Refuge
- State Park
- Wilderness Area

Home Means Nevada

words and music by Bertha Raffetto

'Way out in the land of the set - ting sun, Where the wind blows wild and free, There's a

love - ly spot, just the on - ly one That means home sweet home to me. If you

fol - low the old Kit Car - son trail, Un - til des - ert meets the hills, Oh you

cer - tain - ly will a - gree with me, It's the place of a thou - sand thrills.

CHORUS

Home, means Ne-va - da, Home, means the hills, Home, means the sage and the pines.

Out by the Truck - ee's sil - ver - y rills, Out where the sun al - ways shines,

There is the land that I love the best, Fair - er than all I can see.

Right in the heart of the gold - en west Home, means Ne-va - da to me.

BOOKS

Aldridge, Rebecca. *The Hoover Dam* (Building America: Then and Now). New York: Chelsea House, 2009.

Martin, Ted. *Area 51* (Torque Books: The Unexplained). Minneapolis: Bellwether Media, 2011.

McDaniel, Melissa. *Great Basin Indians* (First Nations of North America). Chicago: Heinemann-Raintree, 2011.

Peters, Jonathan. *Springs in the Desert: A Kid's History of Las Vegas*. Las Vegas: Stephens Press, 2010.

WEBSITES

Nevada State Parks:
http://parks.nv.gov

Nevada Tourism: Welcome to Nevada!:
http://travelnevada.com

Official Website of the State of Nevada:
http://www.nv.gov

Terry Allan Hicks has written books on subjects ranging from the Declaration of Independence to the state of New Hampshire. He lives in Connecticut with his wife, Nancy, and their sons, Jamie, Jack, and Andrew.

Ellen H. Todras is a freelance writer and editor. She has written parts of many social studies textbooks. She also has authored *Angelina Grimké: Voice of Abolition*, a young-adult biography, and other books about the United States. She loves history and enjoys bringing it to life for young people. She lives with her husband in Eugene, Oregon.

INDEX ★ ★ ★ ★ ★ ★ ★ ★ ★ ★ ★ ★ ★ ★ ★

Page numbers in **boldface** are illustrations.